DINOSAURS
STICKER BOOK

Dr. David Norman

Edited by Phillip Clarke
Designed by Reuben Barrance
Consultant: Darren Naish

Illustrated by Bob Hersey, Ian Jackson, Todd Marshall, Luis Rey,
Franco Tempesta, John Woodcock and David Wright

How to use this book

There are over eighty dinosaurs and prehistoric animals in this book. Using the descriptions
and the pictures, match each sticker to the right animal. If you need help, a checklist
and index at the back of the book tells you which stickers go with which entries.

A pronunciation guide is given for the name of most of the animals
in this book. The part in capitals is to be stressed the most.
For example: *Ceratosaurus* (se-rat-o-SORE-us)

You will also find a head-to-tail measurement of each creature, along with the period in which it lived.
Below, you can see when these periods were, and one of the animals that lived in each one.
The abbreviation 'mya' stands for 'millions of years ago'.

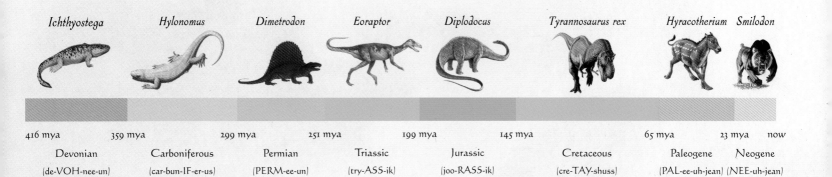

| *Ichthyostega* | *Hylonomus* | *Dimetrodon* | *Eoraptor* | *Diplodocus* | *Tyrannosaurus rex* | *Hyracotherium* | *Smilodon* |

416 mya	359 mya	299 mya	251 mya	199 mya	145 mya	65 mya	23 mya	now
Devonian	Carboniferous	Permian	Triassic	Jurassic	Cretaceous	Paleogene	Neogene
(de-VOH-nee-un)	(car-bun-IF-er-us)	(PERM-ee-un)	(try-ASS-ik)	(joo-RASS-ik)	(cre-TAY-shuss)	(PAL-ee-uh-jean)	(NEE-uh-jean)

Before the dinosaurs

Hundreds of millions of years before the dinosaurs, all animals lived in the water. Eventually, over many generations, their bodies changed and adapted and some of them began to live on the land.

Ichthyostega

(ik-thee-OS-tig-a)
Length: 1m (3ft)
Late Devonian

Eventually, animals with legs developed. They lived on dry land some of the time, but returned to the water to lay their squashy eggs. Today, animals that do this are called amphibians. *Ichthyostega* was an amphibian. It lived mainly in the water and ate fish.

Eusthenopteron

(use-then-OP-ter-on)
Length: 1m (3ft)
Devonian

This fish lived around 375 million years ago. When the water it was living in dried up in hot seasons, it crawled onto land. It had sharp teeth, and strong fins to help it swim and pull itself along the ground.

Diplocaulus

(dip-lo-CALL-us)
Length: 80cm (2ft)
Permian

This creature spent most of its life in the water. It had a flat body and small legs. Its boomerang-shaped head may have helped to stabilize it when it swam in fast-flowing streams.

Seymouria

(see-MORE-ee-a)
Length: 80cm (2ft)
Permian

Seymouria lived mainly on dry land, so its legs were fairly powerful. It was one of a range of early land animals.

Dinosaur ancestors

Millions of years later, animals called reptiles developed. They had scaly skin, and laid eggs that could survive in air because they had protective shells. A group of reptiles called archosaurs (ARK-o-saws) were ancestors of dinosaurs.

Hylonomus

(high-LON-om-us)
Length: 20cm (8in)
Carboniferous

This small, lizard-like creature is one of the earliest reptiles we know about. It had strong ribs and lungs for breathing air, and so was much better suited to living on dry land than the amphibians that came before it.

Pareiasaurus

(pa-ray-a-SORE-us)
Length: 2.5m (8¼ft)
Permian

This ox-sized plant-eater was solidly built, with a tough hide, and bony bumps and knobs on its head. It may have been an ancestor to modern turtles.

Euparkeria

(you-park-EAR-ee-a)
Length: 70cm (27½in)
Early Triassic

Euparkeria was the size of a cat, and its back was studded with small plates for protection. It could probably sprint quickly on its back legs.

Rutiodon

(ROOT-ee-o-don)
Length: 4–5m (13–16½ft
Late Triassic

Rutiodon was a primitive, crocodile-like archosaur. It had a powerful tail and bony-plated skin. Its nostrils were on the raised mound between its eyes. These animals lived in the water and fed mostly on fish.

Sharovipteryx

(sha-rov-IP-ter-ix)
Length: 20cm (8in)
Triassic

This animal was an archosaur-like reptile that probably lived in trees. It seems to have glided using a skin membrane stretched between its tail and back legs.

Big hunters

Theropods (THEER-op-odds) were a group of meat-eating dinosaurs that moved on two legs. The largest ones probably killed their prey with their teeth rather than their claws.

Tyrannosaurus rex

(tih-ran-o-SORE-us rex)
Length: 12m (40ft)
Late Cretaceous

Tyrannosaurus rex was one of the biggest land predators that has ever lived. It had a massive head, and powerful jaws to crush its prey. Its name means "tyrant lizard king" in Latin. It was 5m (16½ft) tall, and fairly heavy, so it could run quickly only in short spurts. Many scientists think it was a relative of modern birds, and that young tyrannosaurs may have had downy feathers.

Allosaurus

(al-o-SORE-us)
Length: 10m (33ft)
Late Jurassic

This large theropod hunted giant sauropods (see page 9). We know this because the teeth marks of *Allosaurus* have been found embedded in an *Apatosaurus* skeleton.

Ceratosaurus

(se-rat-o-SORE-us)
Length: 6m (19½ft)
Late Jurassic

The most unusual feature of *Ceratosaurus* was a row of small, bony plates along its back. It had a horn on its snout, and bony ridges over its eyes. We don't know for certain what the horn was for, but it may have been used by the males for butting each other.

Majungatholus

(mah-joong-ga-THO-lus)
Length: 8m (26ft)
Late Cretaceous

Majungatholus was a theropod whose remains have been found in Madagascar, off the coast of Africa. It hunted plant-eaters such as sauropods. It also seems to have been a cannibal, feeding on its own kind.

Spinosaurus

(spy-no-SORE-us)
Length: 15m (50ft)
Cretaceous

Spinosaurus was unusual because it had spines making a sort of "sail" on its back. Some spines were up to 2m (6½ft) long. This sail may have helped to control the dinosaur's temperature by allowing it to gain or lose heat. Some scientists think it wasn't a sail but a fatty hump, like a bison's, storing energy for times when food was scarce.

Cryolophosaurus

(cry-oh-lof-o-SORE-us)
Length: 7m (23ft)
Early Jurassic

Cryolophosaurus was an *Allosaurus*-like theropod that lived in Antarctica – which was warmer then than now, though it would still have been very cold. The males had a fan-shaped crest which they probably used to attract mates.

Male

Female

Fast runners

Some meat-eating dinosaurs chased their prey at high speeds. They also used their running skills to escape the larger meat-eaters.

Velociraptor

(ve-LOSS-i-rap-ter)
Length: 1.5m (5ft)
Late Cretaceous

This clever dinosaur was probably feathered, and may have hunted in packs. It had a long, curved claw on each foot, which it probably used to grip prey and pierce their windpipes (see also page 16).

Eoraptor

(EE-oh-rap-ter)
Length: 1m (3ft)
Late Triassic

This dinosaur is one of the earliest known. It was a small, fast-moving theropod with three fingers on each hand.

Compsognathus

(comp-sog-NAITH-us)
Length: 70cm (27½in)
Late Jurassic

Compsognathus is one of the smallest known dinosaurs. It was no bigger than a cat and chased tiny animals, mainly lizards, for its food. It used its long tail to balance when running, and it had three clawed fingers on each hand.

Troodon

(TROH-o-don)
Length: 1.8m (6ft)
Late Cretaceous

Troodon was a long-legged, bird-like meat-eater (although it may have eaten plants, too). It had large, forward-facing eyes, and may have been the most intelligent of all dinosaurs, judging by the size of its brain compared to its body.

Coelophysis

(see-lof-EYE-sis)
Length: 3m (10ft)
Late Triassic

This was one of the early meat-eating dinosaurs. It was slender and lightly built, with bird-like feet. It probably lived in groups and fed on young dinosaurs or small lizards.

Megaraptor

(MEG-a-rap-ter)
Length: 8m (26ft)
Late Cretaceous

Megaraptor attacking an Iguanadon

When the remains of *Megaraptor* were first found, its deadly 40cm (16in) sickle claws led scientists to think it was like a huge *Velociraptor*. They now think it may have been a relative of *Allosaurus* (see page 4).

Sinosauropteryx

(sine-oh-sore-OP-ter-ix)
Length: 65cm (25in)
Early Cretaceous

The remains of this small dinosaur were found in China in 1996. It looked like *Compsognathus*, but was covered in fluff or fuzz. This is a very exciting discovery, since it seems to link birds and small theropod dinosaurs closely together. The fluff may be an early version of a feather-like covering.

Gallimimus

(ga-li-MY-mus)
Length: 6m (20ft)
Late Cretaceous

Gallimimus was a very fast, ostrich-shaped dinosaur. It had a long, toothless beak which it probably used to clip leaves from trees. Its back legs were long and powerful, and may have been used for kicking enemies.

Fast runners

The arms of *Deinocheirus*, compared in size to an adult human

Oviraptor

(OH-vi-rap-ter)
Length: 2.5m (8ft)
Late Cretaceous

Oviraptor is Latin for "egg-thief", as the first fossil of this dinosaur was found lying on top of eggs. It is now thought that the eggs were its own, and that *Oviraptor* was no thief, but a caring mother.

Deinocheirus

(dine-o-KY-rus)
Length: unknown, but possibly up to 20m (66ft)
Late Cretaceous

So far, only the massive arms of this mysterious dinosaur have been found. No one knows what it looked like, but it's thought to have been a huge, ostrich-like dinosaur, like a giant *Gallimimus*. The arms are 2.4m (8ft) long.

Deinonychus

(dine-ON-ih-kus)
Length: 3m (10ft)
Early Cretaceous

Deinonychus was a fierce, keen-eyed, smart and fast-moving hunter. It ambushed its prey, stabbing it with large claws on its back feet. There is evidence from fossils that it may have hunted in packs.

Saurornithoides

(sore-or-nith-OI-deez)
Length: 2–3m (6½–10ft)
Late Cretaceous

Saurornithoides had particularly large eyes. This may have meant that it could see better in the dark than other dinosaurs. Experts think it may have hunted small, shrew-like mammals that came out at night.

Giant plant-eaters

The biggest land animals that ever lived were a group of dinosaurs called the sauropods (SAW-ro-pods). They were plant-eaters with very long necks and tails, and they lived in the Jurassic and Cretaceous Periods.

Apatosaurus

(a-pat-o-SORE-us)
Length: 20m (65½ft)
Late Jurassic

This dinosaur was shorter than *Diplodocus*, but much heavier, perhaps weighing as much as 30 tonnes (29½ tons). It used to be known as *Brontosaurus*.

Diplodocus

(dih-PLOD-o-kus)
Length: 27m (88½ft)
Late Jurassic

This dinosaur was surprisingly lightly built, perhaps weighing only 15 tonnes (14¾ tons). It used its whip-like tail to ward off attackers such as *Allosaurus* (see page 4). Its long neck helped it to reach the treetops for leaves to eat. It had a sharp thumb-claw that was probably used for fighting.

Brachiosaurus

(brack-ee-o-SORE-us)
Length: 23m (75½ft)
Late Jurassic

Unlike other sauropods, the front legs of *Brachiosaurus* were longer than the back ones. Its long neck helped it to feed on tall trees. Its nostrils were right on top of the bump on its head. They may have let out hot air to help it cool down as well as breathe.

Supersaurus

(super-SORE-us)
Length: 40m (130ft)
Late Jurassic

Supersaurus was one of the very largest sauropods. It may have been the longest land animal that ever lived. It weighed close to 50 tonnes (49 tons).

Agile plant-eaters

These plant-eating dinosaurs, called ornithopods, were all fast runners that made agile (quick and neat) movements in order to escape predators. They had bird-like feet and tough beaks for biting shoots and leaves.

Ornithopod remains have been found in rocks dating from the Late Triassic to the Early Cretaceous periods. Most of them, like those shown here, stood on their long back legs. They used their short arms for gathering plants together or pulling down branches.

Heterodontosaurus

(het-er-oh-dont-o-SORE-us)
Length: 1m (3¼ft)
Early Jurassic

This dinosaur was distantly related to the ornithopods. It had strong arms with sharp claws and, unusually, tusks in both jaws. It may have used these to dig up roots to eat, to ward off enemies like *Coelophysis* (see page 7), or to display in the mating season.

Hypsilophodon

(hips-ill-OFF-o-don)
Length: 2m (6½ft)
Early Cretaceous

Hypsilophodon had five fingers on each of its short arms and four toes on each foot. It probably used its long, stiff tail to balance while running. Similar small, beaked dinosaurs existed throughout the entire time that dinosaurs lived.

Leaellynasaura

(lee-ell-in-a-SORE-a)
Length: 2.5m (8ft)
Early Cretaceous

Leaellynasaura was a small ornithopod with long legs. It lived in Australia, which was colder then than now. It had big eyes, which would have helped it to see in the dim winter months. *Leaellynasaura* very likely lived in groups.

Muttaburrasaurus

(muht-a-buhr-a-SORE-us)
Length: 7m (23ft)
Early Cretaceous

Muttaburrasaurus, from Australia, was a close relative of *Iguanodon*. The males may have had large bumps on their muzzles, with bright markings to attract mates.

Male

Female

Iguanodon

(ig-WAN-o-don)
Length: 10m (33ft)
Early Cretaceous

This beaked dinosaur had a powerful tail and back legs. It had a long pointed spike on each thumb, which it probably used to defend itself. The other fingers had hoof-like claws, so it could walk on all fours if necessary.

Ouranosaurus

(oo-ran-o-SORE-us)
Length: 6m (19½ft)
Cretaceous

Ouranosaurus was a close relative of *Iguanodon*, but had a broad, flattened beak. It had a structure like a sail on its back to help control its body temperature. As with the *Spinosaurus* (see page 4), this may have supported a fatty hump.

Early idea of an Iguanodon

When the first teeth and bones of *Iguanodon* were discovered, experts thought that it might have been built like a huge scaly rhinoceros, with a bone on its nose like a horn. Only later, when complete skeletons were discovered, did they have enough evidence to realize that this bone was longer, and was really a thumb-claw.

Duck-billed dinosaurs

Duck-billed dinosaurs are also known as hadrosaurs. Their top jaws were flattened at the tip and looked like a duck's beak. Their bodies were very similar, but their heads were all different from one another.

Many had spikes or crests on their heads. These may have helped to make warning noises or to call mates. Different structures would create different noises, so each hadrosaur could make its own sound.

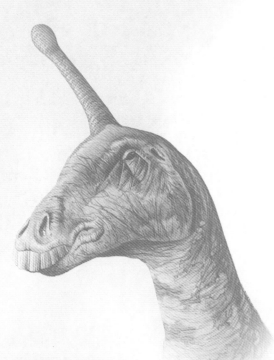

Parasaurolophus

(para-sore-OL-o-fuss)
Length: 10m (33ft)
Late Cretaceous

This dinosaur had an amazing crest made of long, curved, tube-shaped bone. By blowing air through this crest, it may have made trombone-like noises to call mates, scare off rivals, or to warn others that predators were nearby.

Tsintaosaurus

(ching-dow-SORE-us)
Length: 10m (33ft)
Late Cretaceous

Tsintaosaurus, whose remains were found in China, seems to have had a long spike on its head. It was made of solid bone and pointed forwards, a little like a unicorn's horn, although it may have supported flaps of skin. Like all hadrosaurs, it had hundreds of tiny teeth which it used to grind up tough plants.

Hadrosaurus

(had-ro-SORE-us)
Length: 10m (33ft)
Late Cretaceous

Hadrosaurus was the first dinosaur with a near-complete skeleton to be found. It ate leaves from bushes.

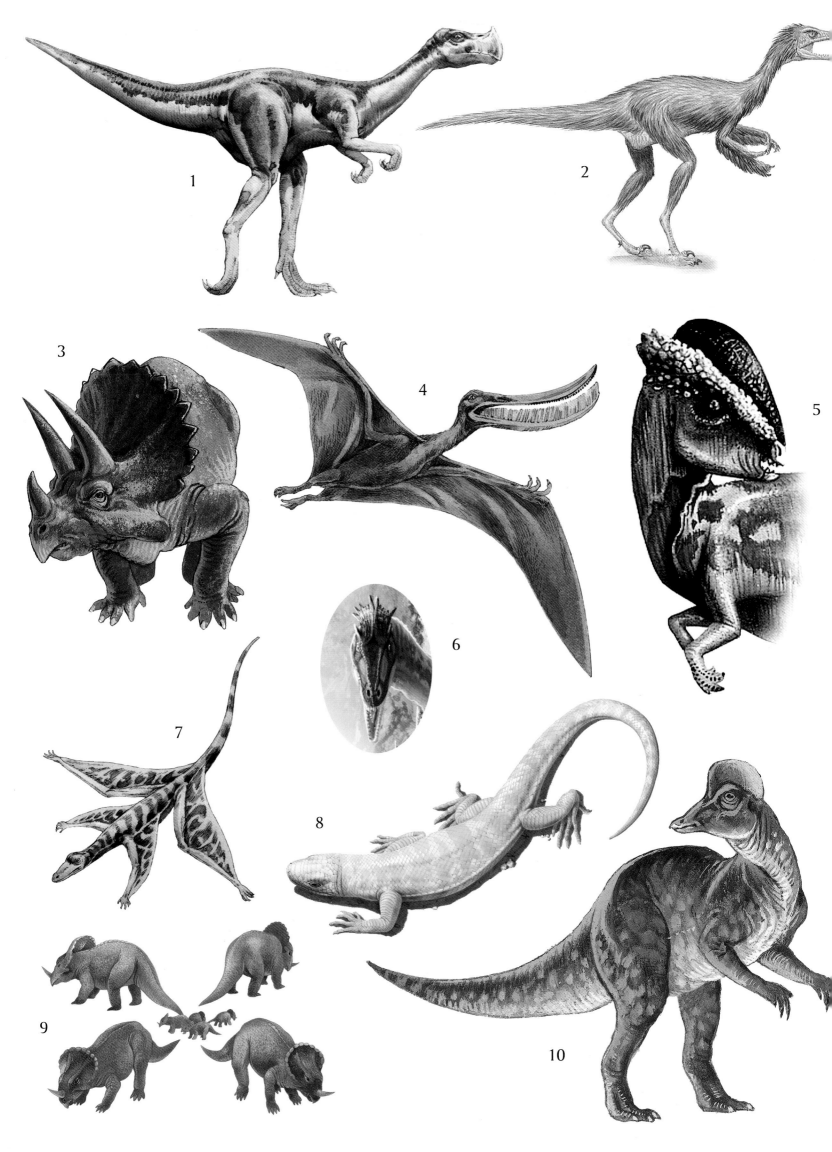

11

12

13

14

15

16

17

18

19

20

30

31

33

32

35

34

36

37

56

57

58

59

60

61

62

63

64

5

66

67

68

69

70

71

Edmontosaurus

(ed-mont-o-SORE-us)
Length: 10m (33ft)
Late Cretaceous

Edmontosaurus roamed in
forests and lived in groups for
protection. It fed on plants and,
despite its large size, could run
quickly on its strong back legs.

Saurolophus

(sore-OL-o-fuss)
Length: 13m (40ft)
Late Cretaceous

This dinosaur had a backward-pointing
prong on top of its head, which may
have been a support for nose pouches.
It may have blown up the pouches with
air, so that it could bellow at rivals.

Kritosaurus

(krit-o-SORE-us)
Length: 10m (33ft)
Late Cretaceous

Kritosaurus had a flat head
with a rounded hump on its
nose. Males may have used this
for head-butting rivals. Females
may not have had this hump.

Corythosaurus

(ko-rith-o-SORE-us)
Length: 10m (33ft)
Late Cretaceous

Corythosaurus means "helmet lizard", after the shape of its
crest. This had many hollow passages inside it, running
from the tip of the dinosaur's nose to the back of its throat.
Some experts believe that these passages may have given
Corythosaurus a strong sense of smell, or that they may
have been used to help it make trumpet-like sounds.

13

Fossil clues

Knowledge about prehistoric life comes from the remains of animals and plants that died millions of years ago. These remains, called fossils, were preserved by being cemented into the rocks in which the dead plant or animal became buried.

Maiasaura guarding its young

Ichthyosaurus skeleton

(ik-thee-o-SORE-us)
Length: 1.8m (6ft)
Jurassic

This fossil *Ichthyosaurus* (see page 21) is very well preserved. Even the outline of the animal's skin can be seen.

Maiasaura

(my-a-SORE-a)
Length: 9m (30ft)
Cretaceous

In Montana, USA, nests made of raised mud have been found, containing fossils of eggs and baby dinosaurs. They belonged to a hadrosaur called *Maiasaura*. It looked after its eggs, and then fed its babies with berries until they were strong enough to leave the nest.

Fossil eggs

The first dinosaur nests to be found were discovered in Mongolia. They contained eggs 15–20cm (6–8in) long. It was thought at first that they belonged to *Protoceratops* (see page 16), but new evidence from other fossils suggests that they belonged to *Oviraptor* (see page 8). Each female laid up to twelve eggs in the sand, in a circle.

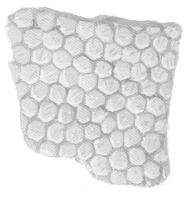

Dinosaur skin

Fossilized impressions of dinosaur skin have also been found, showing that some dinosaurs had pebbly skin. The soft tissue has rotted away, so no one knows for certain what the real skin shades were.

Dinosaur dropping

Fossils of dinosaur droppings are called coprolites. Scientists cut them into thin slices, polish them until they are almost transparent, and then examine them under a microscope. The droppings can show what dinosaurs ate and also the shape of the dinosaur's intestines.

Bone-headed dinosaurs

These dinosaurs had very thick skulls and are known as bone-headed dinosaurs, or pachycephalosaurs (pak-ee-SEFA-lo-saws). They were all plant eaters that moved on strong back legs.

Battling bone-heads

Male pachycephalosaurs
fighting for leadership

Male bone-heads probably had head-banging contests. Two dinosaurs would charge at each other, butting one another's bodies with their heads. They would do this again and again until one gave up. The winner of the fight became the leader of the herd.

Pachycephalosaurus

(pak-ee-sefa-low-SORE-us)
Length: 8m (26ft)
Late Cretaceous

This was the biggest of the bone-headed dinosaurs, and it had the largest bony, dome-shaped head. Its skull was much bumpier than *Stegoceras* (below) and it had lumps and spikes on its nose.

Homalocephale

(hom-a-low-SEF-al-ee)
Length: 2.5m (8ft)
Late Cretaceous

The fossils of this pachycephalosaur, discovered in Mongolia, are some of the best-preserved. This animal had an unusually flat skull, with bony knobs at the sides. Its name means "level head". It also had a very stiff, thick tail.

Stegoceras

(steg-OS-er-as)
Length: 3m (10ft)
Late Cretaceous

Stegoceras was one of the smaller bone-heads, and the first ever to be found. It had a fringe of bony bumps around the back and sides of its head. Scientists think it may have lived in herds, like the other bone-heads.

Horned dinosaurs

Horned dinosaurs, also called ceratopsians, (sera-TOPS-ee-ans) were mostly large and heavy, with horns on their heads and a bony frill around their necks. They all had parrot-like beaks.

Monoclonius

(mon-o-CLONE-ee-us)
Length: 8m (26ft)
Late Cretaceous

From sideways-on, this dinosaur looked similar to a modern-day rhinoceros. It had a single, bony horn on its nose and very small eyebrow ridges.

Pentaceratops

(pent-ah-SERA-tops)
Length: 7m (23ft)
Late Cretaceous

The large frill of *Pentaceratops* extended halfway down its back. It had nose and eyebrow horns, and pointed cheekbones beneath its eyes.

Protoceratops grappling with Velociraptor

Living in herds

Lots of fossil *Monoclonius* have been found lying together. Experts think that at least some of the horned dinosaurs lived in herds. They may also have surrounded their babies to protect them from enemies when threatened. However, there is not yet any solid evidence to support this idea.

Protoceratops

(proh-toe-SERA-tops)
Length: 2m (6 ½ ft)
Cretaceous

Protoceratops was an ancestor of horned dinosaurs such as *Monoclonius* and *Pentaceratops*. It used its strong beak for eating tough plants. One amazing fossil from Mongolia shows *Protoceratops* in a life-and-death struggle with *Velociraptor* (see page 6).

Monoclonius protecting their young

Pachyrhinosaurus

(pack-ee-rye-no-SORE-us)
Length: 4m (13ft)
Late Cretaceous

This horned dinosaur was unusual because it had a short frill and no obvious horns. Instead of a pointed horn on its nose, it had a thick and flattened pad, which gave it an unusual appearance. Only a few skulls of this dinosaur have been found so far.

Triceratops

(try-SERA-tops)
Length: 11m (36ft)
Late Cretaceous

This was one of the largest horned dinosaurs and also one of the last, living right at the end of the Cretaceous Period. The sharp horns around its eyes grew up to 1.5m (5ft) long. It probably charged head-down at enemies, spearing them to death.

Psittacosaurus

(sit-ak-o-SORE-us)
Length: 2m (6½ft)
Cretaceous

This dinosaur was a similar shape to the ornithopods (see pages 10-11). Unusually for a ceratopsian, it walked on its back legs, but probably walked on all fours at times.

Leptoceratops

(lep-toe-SERA-tops)
Length: 2m (6½ft)
Late Cretaceous

Leptoceratops was another unusual horned dinosaur. Rather than being big and heavy, it was small and agile and ran on all fours. Because it could run to escape enemies, it did not need horns to defend itself. It had only a little frill.

Spikes and bony backs

Some plant-eating dinosaurs, called stegosaurs, had large, bony plates sticking out of their backs. Other dinosaurs, called ankylosaurs (ank-EYE-lo-saws), had spikes and bony shields.

Kentrosaurus

(kent-ro-SORE-us)
Length: 5m (16½ft)
Late Jurassic

Kentrosaurus had a long spike on each side of its body, as well as spikes on rows down its back. It probably turned its back on enemies to make an attack difficult.

Polacanthus

(pol-a-KANTH-us)
Length: 4m (13ft)
Cretaceous

This ankylosaur had a broad, shield-like band of bony plating across its hips, and a double row of spines along its neck and tail.

Scelidosaurus

(ske-lid-o-SORE-us)
Length: 4m (13ft)
Early Jurassic

Scelidosaurus was an early ankylosaur. It had a turtle-like beak for close nibbling of low-lying plants. It was the first near-complete fossil dinosaur discovered, in Dorset, England, in 1858.

Stegosaurus

(steg-o-SORE-us)
Length: 8m (26ft)
Late Jurassic

It was once thought that the large plates on *Stegosaurus'* back protected it against enemies. Experts now think that they may have acted as "solar panels", to absorb the heat in sunlight, or radiate it away to prevent the animal from overheating. The group of sharp spikes on its tail (called the thagomizer) was for protection.

Panoplosaurus

(pan-o-plo-SORE-us)
Length: 7m (30ft)
Late Cretaceous

This ankylosaur had simple, leaf-shaped teeth, similar to the stegosaurs, and its jaw ended in a tough, toothless beak. It had spikes along its sides.

Ankylosaurus

(ank-eye-lo-SORE-us)
Length: 4.5m (15ft)
Late Cretaceous

Thick, flexible, bony plates covered the head, neck and back of this dinosaur. Like some of the other ankylosaurs, it had a tail with a chunk of bone welded to the end, forming a club. When under attack, it probably crouched down to protect its soft belly. It also may have swung its tail, giving the enemy a hard whack on the legs, or even breaking them.

Nodosaurus

(node-o-SORE-us)
Length: 6m (19½ft)
Cretaceous

With a name meaning "knobbly lizard", *Nodosaurus'* most distinctive features were the broad bands of rounded, bony lumps across its back. This thick, heavy coat would have acted as protective plating.

Euoplocephalus

(you-oh-plo-SEF-a-lus)
Length: 7m (23ft)
Late Cretaceous

This large ankylosaur had heavy, bony plating on its skin. There were lots of bumps and lumps growing out of it. Thick bone covered its head, like a helmet. Even its eyelids were shielded by bony plates. Its belly appears to have been soft and unprotected.

Flying reptiles

While the dinosaurs lived on land, flying reptiles called pterosaurs (TEH-ro-saws) soared through the skies. They were light creatures, with bat-like wings of stretched, leathery skin. There is good evidence they were covered with short, hairy fuzz.

Pterodactylus

(teh-ro-DAK-til-us)
Length: 20cm (8in)
Late Jurassic

This was a very small, fast-moving pterosaur. It may have snapped insects out of the air as it flew, or probed for worms in shallow water. It would have crouched on all fours when it landed on the ground.

Pterodaustro

(teh-ro-DAW-stroh)
Length: 1.3m (4¼ft)
Early Cretaceous

This South American pterosaur had a very long, curved beak with hundreds of tightly-packed, bristle-like teeth. It used these to filter tiny creatures from the sea.

Rhamphorhynchus

(ram-for-RINK-us)
Length: 30cm (12in)
Late Jurassic

This pterosaur had a sharp beak on its jaw-tips and sharp, forward-pointing teeth to help it grasp fish. The kite-shaped tip of its long tail helped it to steer as it skimmed the sea's surface for prey.

Pteranodon

(teh-RAN-o-don)
Length: 1.8m (6ft)
Late Cretaceous

This pterosaur had huge wings and a long, bony crest on its head. It probably had a pouch like a pelican for carrying the fish it had snatched. It had a short, stumpy tail and no teeth. Its bones were light and hollow which helped it to fly.

Swimming reptiles

Reptiles also lived in the sea during the age of dinosaurs. Some of them looked like dolphins or fish. Others had long necks or huge jaws.

Nothosaurus

(no-tho-SORE-us)
Length: 3m (10ft)
Triassic

This early sea-reptile came ashore to lay eggs. It caught fish with its sharp teeth and had webbed feet for swimming.

Ichthyosaurus

(ik-thee-o-SORE-us)
Length: 1.8m (6ft)
Early Jurassic

Ichthyosaurus was dolphin-like in its shape, and in that it gave birth to live young. It swam like a fish, though, lashing its tail from side to side, rather than up and down like a dolphin. It used its fins to balance and to steer through the water.

Mauisaurus

(mou-ee-SORE-us)
Length: 12m (40ft)
Late Cretaceous

This animal was one of a group of long-necked sea reptiles called plesiosaurs (PLEE-see-o-saws). They swam slowly, probably flapping their flippers up and down like sea turtles, and used quick neck movements to help them catch fish.

Liopleurodon

(lie-o-PLOO-ro-don)
Length: 15m (50ft)
Late Jurassic

Liopleurodon is the largest known member of a group of fierce, short-necked creatures called pliosaurs (PLY-o-saws), relatives of the plesiosaurs. It hunted plesiosaurs and other big sea reptiles, sniffing them out with a powerful sense of smell.

The rise of the mammals

The dinosaurs died out 65 million years ago, as did the pterosaurs and sea reptiles. No one is sure why. One idea is that a giant asteroid landed, causing a huge explosion that led to many kinds of animals dying out.

About half of all animal types did survive, though, including mammals. Mammals have hair, keep their bodies warm and feed their babies with milk. They developed from animals known as synapsids (sin-AP-sids).

Dimetrodon

(dim-EAT-rod-on)
Length: 3m (10ft)
Permian

Dimetrodon was an early, meat-eating synapsid. The tall spines that made the sail shape on its back may have helped to control its body temperature, by absorbing heat from time to time. It had sharp teeth.

Cynognathus

(sy-nog-NAITH-us)
Length: 2m (6½ft)
Early Triassic

This synapsid had some mammal-like features, including several different types of teeth. It had a dog-like look.

Megazostrodon

(mega-ZOST-ro-don)
Length: 8 – 10cm (3 – 4in)
Early Jurassic

Megazostrodon was one of the earliest true mammals. Experts suggest that it was hairy and fed its babies on mothers' milk. It was tiny and shrew-like, and hunted at night for insects and grubs.

Thrinaxodon

(thrin-AX-o-don)
Length: 50cm (20in)
Early Triassic

This creature was even more mammal-like than *Cynognathus*. It had different kinds of teeth, and whiskers on its nose. It may even have had a hairy body, but there is not yet any evidence for this.

Smilodon

(SMILE-o-don)
Length: 3m (10ft)
Neogene

This mammal lived long after the dinosaurs had gone. It existed about 11,000 years ago, during the last ice age, when our planet was very cold. It was fierce, and may have hunted the woolly mammoth.

Woolly mammoth

Length: 6.5m (21ft)
Neogene

This mammal also lived during the last ice age. Its woolly coat and a thick layer of fat kept it warm. The remains of these animals have been found in the permafrost (permanently frozen ground) of Siberia in Russia.

Archaeopteryx

(ark-ee-OP-ter-ix)
Length: 20cm (8in)
Late Jurassic

Archaeopteryx fossil

The first *Archaeopteryx* fossil was found in 1861. The feathers on the wings and tail can be seen very clearly. It had teeth, a long bony tail, and wing claws. Its head and legs were probably covered with scaly skin, like dinosaurs and some modern birds.

This was probably the first bird. It lived when the dinosaurs were still alive, and was related to dinosaurs such as *Velociraptor* (see page 6). It may not have flown like a modern bird, but it could have flapped its wings. It wouldn't have taken off from the ground easily, though, because it couldn't flap strongly enough.

Index and checklist

This list will help you find every dinosaur and prehistoric animal in the book. The first number after each entry tells you which page it is on. The second is the sticker number.

Digital imaging by Keith Furnival

Cover photograph © Roger Harris / Science Photo Library

This edition first published in 2006 by Usborne Publishing Ltd, Usborne House, 83–85 Saffron Hill, London ECIN 8RT, England.
www.usborne.com Copyright © 2006, 2002, 1998, 1993, 1980 Usborne Publishing Ltd.
First published in America 2006 UE